A Reading

18–20

A Reading

18–20

o

Beverly Dahlen

INSTANCE PRESS   *Boulder, Colorado*   2006

Some of this work has appeared previously in the following periodicals and anthologies: *Ironwood, Jimmy & Lucy's House of "K", Gallery Works, North Beach Review, Hambone,* and *The Art of Practice: 45 Contemporary Poets* (eds. Barone and Ganick) 1994 and *American Poets Say Goodbye to the 20th Century* (eds. Codrescu and Rosenthal) 1996.

The author wishes to thank Michael Cuddihy (in memoriam) and all the editors, publishers and friends for their support over the years.

Cover images: Vic Hack
Design: Jaime Robles

ISBN 13: 978-0-9679854-4-2
ISBN 10: 0-9679854-4-7
Library of Congress Control Number: 2006920866

Instance Press books are available from Small Press Distribution,
1341 Seventh Street, Berkeley, CA 94710
1-800-869-7533 www.spdbooks.org
instancepress@yahoo.com

A Reading

– 18 –

I could no more have done that than I could have flown. I was censored deleted hands on   a marked battle. a revised version. why should his life have been saved. he was an old man presumably and fit to die. the others might have gone along with this medium priced heresy   might have made light of it the standard justification. did you see any white shadows there?

our visionaries traipsed to the barn concocting a glorious revolution. I scared myself sitting down. one doesn't necessarily wish to go in the predicated direction. did I owe him that?

a grand slam a yankee pacifist. to initiate him one. one by one by step by perilous step. having arrived there one imagined a bridge across the gulf a possible spanning. a faith so precarious it would have been instantly shattered. a tall narrow window blank light. finally one flees the familiar dead a granted order. healing was hardly the right word the violent word. hungry and yielding to fat.

there in the confines of an obliterated horizon. the lifting mists reveal spectral analysis. if you set that out reading from face to face

o

ordination occurred at the lowest level of intensity. beyond that we were free of the strictures. star wars had gotten in my hair like someone's bonnet of bees. he swarmed to her side, an oily grin lighting up his face. he had all the depth of insincerity, grainy. we had become objects too cool to contemplate. the universal color is a bland gray, a toned down beige. some natural environments seem contrived but that's because their images have been taken away. the camera haunts. we were right to have regarded it as the evil eye.

in fact we frame these events as a camera might. we are already scanning the footage, the raw overlook. it will not occur to anyone to make a film of this, the last moments in the life of an unknown passerby. one assumes he was a man, perhaps young. you would like to brush it aside, believing he did not die in that collision. whatever not spoiling the day a raucous drive in the country. the countryside hereabouts veiled in yards of gauzy fog.

from hence I'd be troubled by a persistent nightmare: something (a chiton) had bitten my hand. I could not hold it. a brain grown teeth sharply recommending the dawn. if this were only a desert the colors would be more accurate.

down in the waves the tidal animals pretend they are having an endless life. when I walked up the stairs I heard a typewriter. she facilitated the dinner. media bring us together with distant events in an illusion that our own lives are not sacrificed. watching somebody else's war.

o

terrorism out of context, a story of murder as light reading. *the civilized way to call it a day.* when people meet at the end of a workweek the content of their speech is the oppression of the boss. who *was* that masked man? the industrial decor of my favorite restaurant, the heating ducts painted red. it would be difficult to name the timeless values when gas pumps had become sacred relics. worshipping at a bowl of gelato. how do you do.

history repeats, the second time around as farce. the third time's the charm. marigolds banked on a slope as part of a scientific plan for erosion control. I don't understand you. read up on it: here's a booklist.

content is what's swallowed: junk food.

here's a list. light up the sky with your faith, everything goes into the memory bank. the bombs bursting in air. it's no more difficult than saying you're going to live till you die. forty-five minutes. where does this road end? somewhere beyond the bird observatory. Rasputin held an onion in his right hand. deadlocked.

Gonick made history, so do I. so do you. drink me.

o

jumping in with both feet speak up. around this survey the wound pales and the true believers polarize in the camps of the intended victims. arch not. can you read between the lines. that space may be widening. what is a complete stop. what leader emerges between the dot and the beginning of the next sentence. where in this breakup does one event called sore home occur to deliver the male prerogative.

it is because we are not bound to an earlier reading that nothing in print is sacred. you may as well bow down before a shopping list. anything earlier than 1950 will be deemed superstitious nonsense. autobiography beware. he is an atheist in a foxhole.

therefore I'd be a shadow freed of former hands and execute this mission of destruction on past lives. there is nothing that can be safely brought in to the arena. the body questions. the Frankfurt school in a loose coalition with strippers and wombats. he raised the antenna and the picture cleared. wherever two or three are gathered together in my name the project prospers. ego is now supposed to have given way to mercy and light. cracks through which you could drive a needle.

whatever was the point of organizing the world in this way: the helpless baby. further evidence: my father thought me up fully armed. no consolation there. where does she arise from the sea or in the mountains beyond reason.

o

all that it's not to deprive one.
No man shall be an idiot for purely exterior reasons.
interiority to flux, crime shamefaced
reaches for a larger napkin to cover the wound.
the definition expands, the lunatic fringe
becomes the entire cloth
I is another a killer
where shall we
take the place of that noun that common thing
the third person, the world
the world equal to *x*
or any letter which may stand for the unknown
a great loss, a damnable mystery
sold for a mess of pottage

and you
impossibly sleeping across the table from me
to secure for ourselves and our posterity
the blessings
how shall I shifter shifting shiftless
be one
a hole a number
any letter might take its place
any pronoun armed to the teeth an absolute construction
any thing
having been buried in a mass grave
how shall we name it the third person
the ragged world
the tattered fronds of the holy ghost

Dear Michael,

It was one of my ideas to speak of the third person as if that stood for the world. In another sense it's a sign of the holy ghost. These two are one: "world without end."

Then I was reading a recent essay of Barrett Watten's which begins: "The world is structured on its own displacement." That seemed to me to be true, and also much of what follows in Watten's piece seemed irrefutable. I read it again and again. I tried to imagine using it, going beyond it. All I could really imagine was quoting it in its entirety. What did I want? the negation of a negation? Watten's work reminded me of all I know to be true: that the world, the self and the other are created out of absence, lack, desire; that "desire is the desire for meaning itself" (I don't know where that quote comes from), that desire is that which by definition can never be fulfilled.

"We make something out of what's missing," Watten writes, "by filling in the blanks, giving our meaning to what has been negated. Such are the limits of art."

So the world is put off, and meaning is postponed indefinitely; this is Derrida's *différance*. It is one of the ~~meanings~~ (as long as I'm being derivatively Derridean) of writing as/an endlessly unfinished work.

o

The third person is Eros, who never appears. It is, as Robert Glück has written, the referent, "the guest who doesn't come."

o

The desire for meaning, to produce meaning, fills me with dread and anxiety. We do not want to hear of another's anxiety; there is nothing we can do with it, nor about it. Anxiety, Freud observes, "corresponds to a libido which has been deflected from its object and has found no employment." An unappeased ghost, incessantly circling. The parodic and diminished double of all that was holy.

"What is originally holy is what we have taken over from the animal kingdom—*the bestial*," Engels wrote in 1882, and since then the hundred years war against what is never quite adequately translated as 'instinctual nature' has brought under the domain of repression the very notion of 'the bestial.' It is slanderous thus to describe the activities, for instance, of death squads in El Salvador. We live in a posthumous world. "Nothing can be compelled from the site of the speaker except the outlines of her form." (Watten)

o

In "Achilles Poem" George Stanley wrote: "We know the body is immortal, but the spirit dies." And now, some twenty years later, Barrett Watten proposes that "'existence' itself must be acknowledged to be on the verge of collapse. There is a residue of faith that another will appear to revive it." That residue. That "trace under erasure." Derrida's gesture: Watten's "drama of existence . . . now in quotes . . . "

o

The writer/speaker rises, as if already dead, to address an other, some second person whose existence is equally problematic. Beyond them lies the world, that matrix which at any moment might be rendered void.

o

The identity of the third person: the father, who is either the father of lies or the author of "existence"—in any case, in whose sign we are constituted. To put the sign under erasure is a gesture, feeble in the circumstances, towards unmasking this father. It marks "his" absence. Any name may stand in this place. The logic is absolute. One may conclude, as Watten does: "The world is everything that is *not* the case."

o

Or else the third person is the mother, whose presence is a kind of rumor.

○

She stands a little to one side, out of focus. She makes up the difference. The *différance*. On account of her the symmetry is disordered, the logic evaded: "She lets it [the meaning] fall in advance."

○

The third person is the child, or rather the child-as-child-of-the-mother. Julia Kristeva notes that "the well-known relationship with an object—which exists only as object of love—is founded only as a third-person relationship: neither *I* nor *you* within a relationship of identification or lust, but *he* (*she*). Love replaces narcissism in a third person that is external to the act of discursive communication. Hence, 'God is love': it is for this very reason that he does not exist, except to be imagined as child for a woman."

○

how may this I *Not I*
displaced an other unspeakable
all that succeeds it a text a "text"
in which nothing the structure of narrative
these old words yr old notions put on
in what putting on causes
laughter

there still there a space
"riant, porous" a world left over
a saving grace? her all
& all that
'scapes naming a middle distance
into which what comes to place her
to take her place

hardly
"feminist"
I'd say *well*
(drawling)
time's yr bloody fool
now what

we'd be one or the other
not so which to overcome
but being that "mother" what a word a mouth
full of it leaning
more or less of it
into it some wind
some "oily rain"

nothing

not a sign of it

coming

BIBLIOGRAPHY

Barrett Watten, "The XYZ of Reading: Negativity (& Diane Ward)" in *Jimmy & Lucy's House of "K"* #1 (Oakland: May, 1984).

Jacques Derrida, *Of Grammatology*, trans G. Spivak (Baltimore: Johns Hopkins University Press, 1977).

Julia Kristeva, "Place Names" and "The Father, Love, and Banishment" in *Desire in Language*, ed. L. Roudiez (New York: Columbia University Press, 1980).

○

June 16 – August 12, 1984

A Reading

– 19 –

to amend is to make up the difference
an uncountable noun
good advice but not several furnitures
filled the space along the west wall
a nightmare like a fiction
not a real dream
pursued along gothic lines stone stairs
the weight of a soul in the balance

cross that out counting
and not counting
the bone china to mother
the gift of retribution

what would it make up
though I have not charity
I'd be as tinkling brass or
field lilies
who are the poor *in spirit*
who walk around with the kingdom of heaven
in their heads

who'd be there counting out *peoples*
kindred in the roofs of their mouths
here is the church
and here is the steeple
mimicking past lives
the ghost of a chance
the productions of time congealing
the trees swaying in the wind
as they do in silent films
at 16 frames per second

over and over a tardy light
resurgent insufferable
until a way was found to repair the shield
our poor spare orbit
among the splayed 'aggregate of
gas, dust, and stars' quoting from
existence the movie
the celestial omnibus parked in the alley
the old conductor an allegory in a child's garden
of verses

the basis of a grave philosophy
whatever we think to think
the 'ghost of a chance' an unearned
speculation
the moratorium on interest
bearing steadily to the north

meanwhile the trees
their mechanical boxes grayed out
the stump of a tooth incised on the tongue
where *poco a poco*
we are returned to the void
piece by piece released to decay
on the verge of resisting
the panic urge to *noli-me-tangere*
the blueeyed doctor bearing down
calm abstracted
rifling the wound

laying up treasures on earth where moth and rust do corrupt
she switched into her substantial marble dress and golden
teeth and earrings   whatever next
in this progress towards *everything*   unfitted
the veiled allusions wafting in the nooks of the afternoon
whilst one was accorded a private tour of the food
stretched out across the room   forgive us
our debts that stringy chorus of unseen voices
wrangling in the open courtyard   'the celebrated
pleasures of the mouth'   *trust*
must be another indulgence of those privileged to wait
in cushioned rooms but the poor believe nothing but pain

and what *to entice* o 'temptation' he laughs
leaning to the left a known word
the lisping Spanish proved out he leaves
for home ahead of time   *Alejandro*
my
no relation   father and citizen
                                                        escapee
as indeed who is not
a replacement

in your old age surrounded by grandchildren bearing arms
for los Estados Unidos   the desiring machine

on account of the bad blood between us
I'd furnish your ears with English
an agent of the state
this is the language God speaks
naturally

no known tongue can capture the necessary lesson
this pit of excavation we call our history
the temptation to *everything* dragging forward
the tortured arguments   the final cause

there at the beginning the blank page the *tabu*
la raza chalked on a board in the kitchen
the interdiction of the north
wind as if the belly of darkness turned
over cows hides fur leaves
their undersides   an edged light
the sounding city a nest of serpents

the logic
of the prohibition of one a detour
where nothing
intervenes absolutely
the end of it
a run of time

fortunes flower
abruptly

not so much the

                    signification

        that would

what's   matter drifting un

    such that we are at least

crowds probably, more than enough
crowds, probably more than enough

            o

September 29 – October 15, 1984

the next thing you know

all the trappings of winter set out on the hillsides new grass
a charitable heart   unabated an old welling
towards the spectacular   a festival of light
how ever the dark resists it we come indoors to the fallen
logs in the fire   the diminished voices

here let the record show
a figure built as it proceeds
a pattern long on justification
short as the days shorten
willy nilly to think of Stein
at the head of the column
weekday service here to stay
wandering among the hyacinths

labyrinths shall we not?
detailing the cuts
to disappear
may in Spanish also be a transitive verb
as 'they disappeared my son'

the interrogative meets a fuzzy blank a settled indifference
a soft defense the unlikeliest events as you'd say the only
creatures in their masks backgrounded all making shine of it
the moon a pillar the children with their mythical names
in the underground the faces of the blind gods stare out
across the tracks the train arrives in a storm of wind
rustling our books and papers together adjusting the headset
wandering *with all the biblical antecedents of that choice.*
thus I use you.
the exact price the bird of prey gnawing at the vitals
the renunciation of pleasure on the way to grasping it
the perception of hands in the creation of categories
bestowing on things their –*hood*edness
as a quality or manner such as velvethood or cuphood
so I came into wordhood at an early age sitting right here
don't you suppose we can speak of such nervous organizations?
and now a second cure appears and flows in the path of least
resistance that rebel and thief Prometheus emulated far and wide
a little learning is a dangerous thing who would renounce that
power once procured?

awake at dawn underscore that balmy and listless sinister image.
a tropical storm standing in the way weather permitting. walk out
gathering execration review the setup one last time nipping
into winter's weakness. nothing follows.

Even if we ignore its merits as a work of literature,
the book seems destined to create controversy.

no error. she was sitting above the shelf someone said what nice
perfume but she wasn't wearing any a wholly resistible object.
downpurse relevant wind a stone in the head on which to strike
the rhythm. a world demystified and made over a new theory of
ghosts. beam me up.

of the parts rational of the whole mad my voice bouncing off the
moon. just here she said you go into hyperspace.

renegade information gatherers select a code. recombinant DNA
working close to the bone reset the eye. hand to mouth resuscitation
standard English in disarray.

orange flower water the soup's in us. the captured stick thrown
over the edge of the cliff numbers of ghosts multiply. the space
in the train taken up with drumming. against the background of
industrial waste the nostalgia for the tribal.

burning up the distance
listening in to Santa Fe
you could be anywhere south north

can we speak of the local a day in anybody's time zone nights
tipping toward the solstice hemispheres of execution remote
events written in the fossil record written in the stars
remote execution of events speechless for the luxury of life
on one continent

for the luxury of life on one continent
Africa *thrawn*
Asia *thrawn*
the mythical Americas on the verge
a storm of penitence arises
giving the devil his due

tall in the saddle Armageddon's cowboy
rides out the night
workers of the world unite

o

November 25 – December 9, 1984

having the last word the erotic angel stretches its feathers
the celebrated shepherds recollected as pranksters
and one a thief in that light
whose wife is brought to bed of a lamb
and later suffers the ignominy of discovery

however in our world the twisted gates of the secular
oppose an earlier practice the lines down the wondering
shepherds no more our progeny than the little lamb
who made thee in an uproar of sacrifice
a cut above the others living to eat
our hearts out away there in a manger

the social fabric knit with nylon
the perfect everlasting triumph of
that *God-damned crook and fugitive Robert Hathall*
whose life of crime resembles our own
a spare part an elaborate dumb show

sheltering tough thought in exchange for the thickened plot
the deliberate colors of the fall from grace in a frosted glass
an eternal winter sunset qualified by artifice
by the hairs on her chin dowdy gray
by sexual ambiguity by the refusal to be the classic straight line
by prickly holly thorns below south the sun in the shape
of a rooster's foot inching towards Lapland
where the witches live

upon whom the sun has gone down

quoted on the bare bricks of Market Street
is it the end yet said my grandfather dying
darkness is all *Were*
proud? Of what? To buy

a thing like that.

lo where she enters the rubbishy unregarded field.

the aitch dropped
the weaving spiders come
the domed skull a seacave
the headlands the mouth of the river
filling and falling
crouched in the animal kingdom
to whom do we owe our lives
the visible pulse in the wrist
the waste of fields and forests
blooming in the market pages as *agricultural production*
as *development of natural resources*

the serious powers of old are now portrayed almost exclusively as
women and children; the masculine angel, fear not, is become a cute
fat infant, wingéd cherub

the descendent powers ours
tin horn
toy drum
but soft here comes my mother now
that moth stuttering across Rachel's page

what thoughts these are I think I know
    :   here's a poetry lesson. what's 'unnatural' word order that
Pound's always complaining about is what sticks in the memory,
another mnemonic device which, until so recently, distinguished the
poem from ordinary conversation
writ by hand: an archaism
I ate the plums: wrong tense
the drift of nothingness, the spectacular, each individual plank
whirling in the explosion, walking away from it, the history of movies,
the horrors of bourgeois life

lax-ear'd
father Ricci posing as a Chinese monk
persons of no definite employment given to bewilderment
outrage and terror over and over
we love to hate *modern* art
see what the boys in the back room will have
see what's here
another new year
tea roses
total allout apocalyptic destruction a cliché
a long white blank
the still point of the turning world

I marking time
the events of the past half century
o unhappy century the ruin of childhood
a bourgeois custom or invention
shot down in flames
the human universe behaving as if it had had a prolonged unhappy
                              childhood
                         upon my soul

Ezra: those 'dim lands of peace.' yerse.

dim lands of peace. dim lands of peace. dim lands of peace.
sometimes the memory of something, place or room, returns so vividly,
unexpectedly, as if I were hallucinating the interior of my father's car,
say, in 1946, or when did he sell the old Plymouth, the green one,
'going to see a man about a horse,' earlier, making the trade for it,
were we really to have a *horse*? and where would we keep him and
shall we have a buggy too

autobiography, memory and mechanisms of concealment
that fantasy or wish to sit up all night with her exhausting
one another with talk conceals
o *you* know what
lavish passion in the absence of a mother
impressing *conscripting* language into the service
of repression

Repeated
   evidence has proved that it can live
on what can not revive
      its youth. The sea grows old in it.

                              ○

December 9 – 30, 1984
January 1 and February 18, 1985

letting the book fall closed too sleepy to read the last three pages. voices consume my head the hallucination that someone has called my name I start up and switch off the light. conversations whisper around me on the bus mixing with the drone of the motor. who can be awake at this hour traveling towards the rim of Wyoming.

I suddenly saw that date as 1982 1. the first human ancestors are known to have lived between four and three million years ago. they walked upright had a highly cooperative social order were short in stature and old at thirty. the females not yet women made up the difference achieving a birth rate unmatched by their estrus-bound cousins. it would be wrong to personalize them wrong to be teleological. yet these bones instruct us in a fate so close to our own that 'the final overlay drawing in a sequence like this is somewhat of a shock.'

here then is his solo described in the first quarter. she had
fallen short of the mark. the 'squamous mind' visualizing money.
the quantities are uncertain tied to time. the time money space
equation. the world heats up to the tune. and carries it bodily away.

in the solo flight of Paul Gonsalves a man blows hard on the future.
there are among others keeping time the elegant Duke.

plus fours ruling the infernal regions. simultaneously incapacitated
drawing a line through a line.

living partly in America and partly in the snow she traveled
around the top of the world landing in the first place by a
throw of the dice. what was not autobiographical was the art
part. still these movies would tell a story barely concealed.
did she leaving the plane consider her life well-spoken well-acted?
coolly she sat there pronouncing judgment on what had already
been a twenty-year career.

and what would I recalcitrant dissolving into a nest of thorns?
hardly more keeper more proper among 'the most contemptible . . .
the most miserable:' *thrawn* translates *abject* not English not a verb.

mourning becomes etcetera
somewhere stepping across that line
dividing Europe from Asia
milk from cream
the sun coming up on the late world.
the sacrificial victims of the Bay Bridge the Golden Gate
literally the misstep into the void the fall into concrete
the crushed skull these far-flung monuments
on which death drives the shady cycle
to work   26 men
in the construction of the Bay Bridge
lettered A through Z and signed away
congealed in the product literally I say
stepping out the body alienated in labor
nothing
nothing is ours that another has not died for.

°   "In all, twenty-four workmen were killed, some by dynamite explosions
    deep in the rock foundations, some by falling from the towers or the
    roadway into the bay."

                                   —Richard Halliburton
                                   Book of Marvels (*The Occident*)

whether the focus of the orange was too great the power of the sun
provided little flowers the opportunity to grow up and become
the world's first inventions for the interested parties of the first part.
we automatically transferred the payments into his account after
the signing of the bill. our trappers caught this ghost when he
wandered into the highlands. for over a century, his office
had been located on Main Street.

the poetry center. when the light's on the words glow. when the time
is scared the nights take on an evil appearance. the river mouth
was south of Castro.

low. a word baited. and hooked. dragging the floor of the ocean.
ancient bacteria adapting to a life in pools hotter than boiling.
this increases our chances.

a slip of the tongue thought's slippage a bald-faced lie
a slip of a girl tiny immaculate a foreign horn
burning her buttons tousled in thin air
foot-shod retriever 'coarse materiality'
dragging a poem up by its roots shrieking
mama mama 'the universal cry' a voiced labial
sucking breathing
and then a full stop

eight others in the periphery. far fields, the cannery gone on strike.
what more could you want? a life in the body?
not hauling in all those bits towards immortality.
teaching him the life of the mind. this will hurt you stretching out.
the cat arches and tentatively displaces the moth departing
this world in patterned flight
over the garden now
paired white
the highlands of summer
stuttering an unexpected word

there he is
I was waiting for you
beyond analysis

an hour has gone by
and two minutes
the dictionary dances in a new silver dress
these are my books my house to bestow on him
something which does not fit
a rhymed couplet
going together he pinned the tip
we'd pull ourselves through the sky-hole
but one was left behind wandering on the ice
a monster fit to inhabit those northern regions

and there
there I would go and make my home
a broom you said   corky
corvidae   the crow   also
cuervo   buzzard
our names   unto this end

    inscribed

○

February, March, and July, 1985

A Reading

— 20 —

Redundancy is an antidote to psychic noise Ted says and writing it now I wonder can that be part of the poem or I'm starting to worry what's part of the poem like Spicer who seems to be fussy about that all the time what's in the poem and what's not what you can bring in and can't how old that feels to me now how long I've thought of that not wanting it never occurred to me to credit Spicer now there's a source of thought which I must credit and that's to poor old Spicer paranoiac boob old false face lumbering, something about the raw and the cooked, bulges, and what you could put into that sack and maybe watch it squirm out to the edges the poem a sack of kittens to be drowned. reading Spicer that's morbid his morbidity one side of that affects me strongly something at the boundary of civilization someone who lots of the time was beyond the pale.

Well, yes but where *do* babies come from? Is this the same as asking where poems come from? The child says mom where do babies come from and she says well honey you see a man and a woman yes I *know* that but where do babies *come* from? You might as well say the stork brings them or that poems are transmitted via some radio in the head from Mars. Is this mystification? An argument here as well with Haraway's cyborg myth which abjures an account of origins when after all she explicitly credits the invisible silent machines around us as the ironic parodic triumph of the father. If so, what's the origin of the father. Children that we are, we want to know where babies come from. Necessarily we must account for the father.

o

a dream in fact sprawling event
tincture
the roses gaudy as if
Gaudi the movie not the talk
        dotted gray spiral

the social relations of the mind's eye

in Spicer that wall of water not so much impenetrable as

        there's a gorgeous moon rising just now
        very big and heavy and squat on the edge
        of the hills and the freeway arches
        beneath it with cars zooming under it
        you can see the vast long trail of red
        lights like a tail and the moon ripens
        and rises up the tree of the sky and
        a monkey plays in it and the air settles
        around it into dark blue night and
        everything begins to be blue and silver
        even the moon which had been a violent
        orange hanging above the bay like a threat

if on a bright summer day the whole edge of work were supported by
a ridge of fog

and one knows oneself to be null and void and without redeeming
social significance

and all one's relations are poisoned

and all one's responses are purely mechanical & you might as well
have stayed home and gone to bed because it certainly is an illness &
you might as well have the dream as the reality & you might as well
plead guilty at once and pay the fine and go to jail the only honorable
place to be

when the whole edge of the world, of the known world is spread with
the fine dust of nausea

& mechanical disgust and shame

& you might not know it but
there it is, death to the other
I wish you ill and suffering.

all this was once open fields
and farmlands where I sit the
original land grant of the De
Haro family the Potrero the
meadows of the mission the
windows of the new store o a
couple of blocks up the hill

mention the forerunner
rocking in the shade of his front porch
leaning over the rail spitting tobacco juice into the stripéd
leaves of the laurel
there on Fremont Street beside the alley
        among the steeps
        inclined his head and
        doffed his hat to be kissed
        on the shiny skin of his hairless skull
whatever he thought of his American grandchildren

I thought the only other person more stern and distant was God
his set jaw gray with stubble   frankly a man as filthy as death who
ate fish heads and eyes and all boiled in milk and wretched potatoes
and tough rye bread

these gaudy primates dressed in the rags of the new bewilder
the finest distinctions in the course of a minute or two. fine
in the sense of subtle.

fine-tuning the blunt instrument produces spectacular results.
I mean in the sense of circus. the eyes of Texas are upon you.

I mean Texas in the sense of extremes. the blunt instrument.
the comedy as well as the banality of evil. I mean in the sense
of place. that high and windy moral tone.

o

March 25 and August 3 – 15, 1986

admitting pessimism the crack in the back door.
taking that logical tone of voice with me as in
don't take that logical tone of voice with me who do
you think you *are* anyway? here follow lists of possibilities.
as free for all and unsupported by parallel construction.
the short admonitory sentence fragments of advertising
as do it. now. the request or command indeed the imperative
the order from which you is missing but understood the subject
as you I mean *you* do it. now. to make the case for personalization
a computer generated letter with your very own name on it falls
out of the envelope. if you aren't convinced read this.
read it anyway. an appeal to reason. enough to try your soul.
as a special added incentive a sealed packet of unretouched
photographs included posted this warning do not enter this
house.

that bank of windows opened inward like louvers
and a stiff breeze was dancing the curtains around
so I got up and pushed shut the lowest one nearest me
and L. came into the room and said don't anybody go
so I stayed in my chair in front of the fireplace.
from there I had a different view of the windows
those that were in the side wall and not in front of me.
this was probably the one time I had been in that house
and the weather was hot but night with vague shapes of
trees moving around and the floor was high gloss yellow wood
and everything else was white except some of the curtains
were dark red and I was looking up through the windows
at the tops of the trees waving around thinking aloud
good God I couldn't have done that but laughing in
disbelief and satisfaction like someone who's just
drawn a lot of money out of the automatic teller
at their suburban bank in the middle of a pleasant day
and they go off to spend it not even thinking how much
they deserve it.

everything goes smoothly. you say the perfect thing and you
remember everybody's name. no one seems uncomfortable everyone
seems relaxed and you seem bright and charming. no one
mentions the weather which is controversial or the food
which is plentiful. you walk down the dock thinking
o yes the material basis of reality the cornerstone of
philosophy wasn't it just too pretty. pretty hard or easy
that uninflected tongue that develops a taste for consistency.
much machinations. then we finally get to a place where
there's big water that goes up and down. the boat stands
on its side and the gray hulks in the haze. we salute
the triangular shadow that follows us. that it shall not walk
on dry land is an axiom of mental health. that you believe
in the flight of airplanes proves it. the whole world
was a lackey in his hands.

we were sitting in the skirts of the church with a wicker picnic
basket among us and the floor came up through the gloom to meet me.
the grain stretched out one way and the seams were melded like waves.
the fresh graves loom sharply. the church itself bears a share
of misgiving now that the damage is done. you might have camped
out on that peak in Darien but consider the weather the flies
that ironic tone. for sale around the corner Big Ben booms out
over the water. not every Latino loves magic realism. the
celebrated penchant for the cheap and easy life is nowhere
more belied. those crude bones wrapped in your secondhand jeans
are as unrepentant as any bizarre saint or martyr who never
stepped in the same river twice. increment is all. death
is never timely. history is in eternity. my hands are tied.

after a decent interlude the appeal started again a steady
hammering in the eaves troughs of the State Department
before the rainy season began. the evidence was stiffened
by an eyewitness account of unusual proportions and it
was popularly believed that the borders were breached
in a corresponding tone of voice. however the vote was
inconclusive and the election was reshuffled in favor
of frequent dictators. there will always be someone
who fills the bill. children bathing their bloody stumps
in backcountry creeks will dub him uncle but they mature
more quickly in tropical climes. confirmation awaits
inspection by international teams of authorized observers.
it was a dark and stormy night. someone knocked at the door.
thunder muttered morbidly and the tossing trees were fitfully
lit by convoys grinding up the road. in this outpost of
civilization we are once again testing the theory of the hero
who must be invincible since (a) he was born an orphan and or
(b) he was born the youngest son and (c) he is a very foolish
fellow. since appearances are deceiving he will submit quite
willingly to your questions. penetrating his rustic innocence
as a sinister disguise your obligation is clear. he will be
dispatched along with his family and livestock in the ritual
happy ending. tune him out. have another beer.

let's take a moment for mystification. it's the *fort/da*
sensation all over again. when are the grownups coming
home to rescue us. that bromide bids fair on the auction
block of cynicism. if the child were the father of the man
then T.V. is the father of the child. someone's in the kitchen
with Dinah.

supposing your mother was the goose that laid the golden egg.
if you were the daughter of Midas you might have the sense
to run in terror from his incestuous touch and thereby avoid
the consequence of his pathology. but women were ever deceived
by the lascivious temptation to horn in on art. painting past
the prime Hamlet's mother hove into view. she'll be part of
the body count later in the play but for now she fluffs up
the action. she's hardly far gone enough to be grotesque
but she's seriously overripe. there might just be the tiniest
microscopic spot of rot near the stone though the surface is
intact as a photograph.

verisimilitude is after all a problem in fiction. it demonstrates
our boundless need for belief in the coherence of systems. we
never notice it unless it fails. then we write contemptuous
letters to the author citing the anachronisms. surely the
old man was capable of distinguishing truth from poetry else
what's a conscience for?

o

August 9 – 14, 1986